Job Interview Tips
For Winners
12 Key Ways To Land The Job

Job Interview Tips
For Winners

12 Key Ways To Land The Job

STEVEN FIES

Job Interview Tips For Winners

12 Key Ways To Land The Job

Copyright © 2015 by Steven Fies

All rights reserved. With the exception of quotes used in reviews, this book may not be reproduced or used in whole or in part by any means existing without express written permission from Steven Fies.

Edited by Steven Fies
Published by Steven Fies
United States of America

Electronic Edition: December 2015
Library of Congress Control No.: 2016901516
ISBN: 978-1519709806

For Anyone Searching For Their Dream Job

Contents

Introduction 1

Why I Wrote This Book 5

1. Dress for Success 9
2. Practice Good Posture 11
3. Arrive Ten Minutes Early 15
4. Maintain Eye Contact 19
5. Practice Common Interview Questions 22
6. Thoroughly Research the Company 27
7. Prepare Intelligent Questions to Ask 29
8. Plan Your Transit Route in Advance 33
9. Know Your Strengths and Weaknesses 35
10. Learn How Body Language Affects Communication 41
11. Follow Up with a Prompt "Thank You" 47
12. Have a Balanced View of the Outcome 49

Conclusion 53

Introduction

Welcome to *Job Interview Tips For Winners*! Congratulations on your purchase, you are now just pages away from mastering twelve important interviewing skills.

Before getting started, be sure to grab my *Pre-Interview Checklist* from my personal blog:

http://www.stevenfies.com/job-interview-tips-for-winners-checklist/

This is a great one-page document to keep on hand for the "big day" – and will help you remember some key things you should do two hours before, and fifteen minutes before an interview.

Now, let me give you a little background. I have been a job seeker a number of times throughout my life, so I understand what it's like applying for jobs - and how critical it is to interview with excellence.

Currently, I am a business consultant who advises human resources departments on selecting and retaining the right employees. Because of this, I have a good working knowledge of what it takes to land a great job.

This book is packed with critical information, but short enough to get through in one focused sitting. This is because you should spend the majority of your time applying for jobs and preparing for interviews, not reading unnecessarily dense books on the subject. By trimming the fat, you will be able to learn what's important and get down to business more quickly.

By the way, when you're done with this book I would be forever grateful if you leave an honest review online. Loved it, hated it - whatever. It would be great to get your feedback because this helps me as an author tremendously.

Furthermore, I invite you to join my newsletter at www.stevenfies.com for a chance to preview my future books at no cost.

Thank you for purchasing *Job Interview Tips For Winners* and please enjoy the read.

Why I Wrote This Book

There are several reasons I wrote this book. One reason is that I myself had a tough time finding a job when the economy crashed in 2008, when I was fresh out of college. Even though I had a shiny new degree from top-ranked UC San Diego, there was nothing easy about securing employment in the months that followed.

Therefore, the first reason I wrote this book was to pass on all the knowledge I gained from trial and error, in hopes that it might help even *one* person who is in a tough spot one day like I was.

Now let's fast forward to today.

I've held a number of great jobs since then, worked my way into management, and now own my own business. [My current business](#) is in the area of consulting human resource personnel and executives on managing talent (hiring the right people, building great teams, improving communication, etc.).

Because of this, I've had the opportunity to learn quite a bit about how organizations make hiring decisions, and I think it's only fair that I pass on some of that information to you - my reader, and most likely an active job seeker in today's complex job market.

Perhaps the most compelling reason I wrote this book, though, is because of my desire to effect positive change in the corporate world.

Current research shows up to 80% of employees are dissatisfied with their jobs. This is bad news for everyone, because it means workers are unhappy and employers are losing productivity. We also know the average employer only has a 50% chance of hiring the right person when using traditional methods for evaluating its candidates. This leads to an incredibly high number of mismatched jobs each year in the United States and beyond.

It's important that you don't wind up in a mismatched job. While there's more to a great job match than acing your interview, understanding how to interview properly is certainly the first step. It would be a shame if a great job passed right by you because you made a simple mistake during the interview process, leading you to settle for a mismatched job somewhere else as a result.

Let's make sure that doesn't happen. Read on to sharpen your interviewing skills and give yourself the best possible shot at success.

1. Dress for Success

Dressing for success may seem obvious, but apparently it is not - we hear stories all the time of would-be candidates who show up to interviews looking less than professional.

Unless told otherwise, **plan to wear business professional attire** to all of your interviews.

Additionally, make sure you check off the following items:

- Hair is done and has been cut recently.
- Teeth are brushed and breath is fresh.
- Your face is freshly shaven, or beard is neatly trimmed (if you're a male).
- Go light on the cologne/perfume if you use it.
- Shoes are polished and without scuffs.

Last but not least, look at yourself in the mirror before leaving for your interview. Make sure you look sharp, and if possible, ask a friend to do a quick double-check of your appearance.

When you arrive at the interview, you may bring in a nice looking briefcase, handbag, or folio. However, don't bring food or coffee into your interview unless it's offered to you by the hiring manager during the interview itself.

2. Practice Good Posture

If you already have great posture, then this is an easy one for you. However, most of us do not have such great posture. Many of us hunch over computer screens and keyboards for eight or more hours per day, so it's tough to maintain an upright and confident posture.

If this describes you, then *now* is the time to start working on your posture. Having excellent posture conveys confidence, accountability, and self-assurance. Such nonverbal cues may seem superficial, but they have a greater impact than you might imagine.

Body language experts know that nonverbal communication (such as posture) conveys accurate messages about a person's inner state of mind. By demonstrating an open and strong posture, you convey that you are sure this job is the right fit for you - hands down. On the other hand, hunching over may suggest that you have uncertainty about your qualifications for the role.

One way you can practice excellent posture is to use "power poses." Raising your hands overhead with clenched fists such as a marathon runner might do after winning a race is a great one to try - spread your feet out to shoulder-length distance apart from one another, lift your chin, put a smile on your face, and raise your hands overhead. Now hold this for two full minutes. According to research, this gives you a measurable testosterone boost while decreasing levels of stress hormones in your blood stream.

Once you're done holding the pose, you will naturally maintain a more confident attitude and better posture for a good twenty or thirty minutes afterwards.

Therefore, this is a great exercise to practice immediately before an interview - but also throughout the day leading up to it, and even on a daily basis even when you don't have an interview. Slowly but surely, your posture and confidence levels will increase, and eventually they will become a habit if you stick with it… and once they become a habit, you will not need to concentrate on it anymore - it will be automatic!

3. Arrive Ten Minutes Early

This should be a no-brainer, but much like dressing for success, it's apparently not obvious to everyone. There are a number of reasons to arrive a few minutes early to an interview.

First, something could happen on the road that will cause a delay. By building in some extra time as a buffer, you can ensure that you still arrive on time even if something comes up.

Furthermore, it makes a good impression to arrive to any in-person meeting on time or a few minutes early. It sends a message that you have your act together, are an accountable person, and that you respect the other person's time.

Arriving late for an interview is a surefire way to destroy your chances at landing the job, unless there is an extremely compelling reason to hire you.

Since the interview is the time when you're supposed to put your absolute best foot forward, arriving late is a poor sign of things to come. How can a hiring manager trust that you will show up to your job on time, meet deadlines, and comply with basic policies and procedures if you couldn't even make it to your first meeting on time?

Additionally, arriving a few minutes early gives you the opportunity to do some last-minute preparation. If you need to use the restroom, arriving early means you'll have time to go. If you want to review some last-minute notes on the company, you'll have time to do this. On the other hand, arriving right on time or late means you'll be scrambling, and it will put you at a psychological disadvantage.

Remember - **always show up on time or early to interviews.**

4. Maintain Eye Contact

Someone who can maintain good eye contact will be perceived as trusting, open, confident, and self-assured. Eye contact communicates a sense of confidence, and it sends a nonverbal message that you have nothing to hide.

By contrast, poor or shifty eye contact tends to communicate the opposite - that you are not trustworthy, not confident, and that you may have something to hide. Some people will even assume someone who makes poor eye contact is lying or has something wrong with them. True to form, many body language experts have noticed such traits in known liars.

Maintaining eye contact can be tough, though, can't it? Maintaining steady eye contact with someone else is a real chore if you're not used to it, and it can feel quite intimidating at first. With practice, though, you can become very good at maintaining eye contact. It's important to do this while listening *and* while speaking, too.

Strong eye contact while *listening* to someone else shows that you are paying attention to them, hearing what they are saying, and that the content of their speech matters to you. It validates their existence in the context of your conversation and connects them to you in that moment. Not maintaining eye contact sends a message that you are not paying attention, and that you might be bored with what the other person is saying. This can hurt their feelings and diminish their confidence in your ability to perform well in a job.

Strong eye contact while *speaking* to another person shows confidence in your message and demonstrates that you are trustworthy. Interestingly, people who maintain great eye contact while speaking are assumed to better know what they're talking about than those who don't, and are less likely to be challenged on their statements.

To practice maintaining eye contact, grab a friend, co-worker, or family member, and take turns talking to each other. The key, though, is to maintain eye contact longer than you normally would. For an extra challenge, sit in silence and look into each other's eyes for as long as possible. Most people will feel very uncomfortable after just 15-20 seconds, but you should continue practicing until it feels natural to hold eye contact for a minimum of 1-2 minutes.

Just as sports players practice plays on the field, practicing eye contact like this will make it more natural and automatic to do it in real life - including during interviews, when it really counts.

5. Practice Common Interview Questions

This is something too few people do, and then they are caught off guard when the hiring manager asks them a tough question during the interview. *"Tell me a time you failed or made a mistake at work, and what you learned from it…"*

The Muse posted a great article that features 31 common interview questions, with advice on how to answer each. Our best advice is to spend considerable time thinking through the answers you would give to such questions, and then practice out loud in the mirror (or with a partner). Practice until you can look yourself, or your partner, in the eye and comfortably provide an answer to each question.

Here is a list of 25 common questions you can start practicing immediately:

1. Why do you want this job?
2. Where do you see yourself in 5-10 years?
3. Why do you want to leave your current company?
4. What can you offer us that nobody else can?
5. Are you willing to relocate or travel?
6. Tell me about an accomplishment of which you are very proud.
7. Tell me about a time you made a mistake, and how you corrected it.
8. Why should we hire you?
9. Why are you looking for a new job right now?
10. Tell us about your resume and education.
11. Tell me how you handled a tough situation at work.
12. How would you deal with an angry or irate customer?
13. What are your strengths? Weaknesses?

14. What are your salary and/or benefits requirements?
15. Tell me about a time when you went above and beyond the requirements for a project.
16. Who are our biggest competitors?
17. What was your biggest failure, and what did you learn from it?
18. What motivates you and gets you out of bed in the morning?
19. Tell me about a time when you disagreed with your boss.
20. How do you handle pressure at work?
21. What is the name of our CEO/President?
22. What are your long-term career goals, and how does this job fit into them?
23. If I called your last boss right now and asked him what is an area that you could improve on, what would he say?
24. What are some of your leadership experiences?

25. What's more important, work-life balance or staying late to finish the job? Why?

People sometimes ask, "What's the best answer to these types of questions?" The best answers to these questions are the ones that are *honest*.

Be yourself and be honest, and you'll do alright. If you try too hard to make yourself out to be someone you're not (for example, by lying about where you'd like to be in your career 5-10 years down the road, just because you think it's what they want to hear…), you'll probably get caught in the act, or worse – you might get the job even though it's a poor match for you.

Even if it may seem at the time like getting the job offer is the most important thing, believe me when I say it's not. What's most important is making sure the job is a great fit both ways. If it's not, your performance is bound to suffer and you may end up being miserable as a result.

6. Thoroughly Research the Company

The logic here is simple: if you're applying for a job somewhere, presumably it's because you have researched the company and discovered that you'd love to work there. Expect to be asked some questions about the company during your interview, and to provide your reasons for wanting to work there.

You don't necessarily need to conduct the same level of research that you would for a final exam in college, but you should have a pretty good handle on the basics.

What industry are they in, who are their competitors, who is on the leadership team, and what are current employees saying about the company on websites like Glassdoor? What was it that initially attracted you to the company, and why did you decide to submit yourself for consideration?

You might consider looking into the company's public stock announcements and reports (if they are a publically traded company), and/or reading the company's blog to get an idea what's going on with them in the present moment. Some people will even subscribe to Google Alerts, such that they can become notified when there's new news on the company in question - keeping them totally up to date in the days leading up to the interview.

We recommend doing enough research initially to determine you have an interest in applying for the company, and then once your interview has been scheduled, spend at least a few hours conducting additional research to solidify your knowledge prior to the interview.

7. Prepare Intelligent Questions to Ask

The truth about interviews is that they should always be two-way. Our culture has fallen into a pattern wherein the typical employer screens and qualifies the candidate, but not the other way around - and this is part of the reason dissatisfaction in the workplace is hovering around 80%.

Even if an employer believes a candidate is well-qualified and hires them, the job match may still be poor if the candidate discovers the company, its culture, or its leadership isn't a good fit for them in the long haul. Besides, what's the point of hiring someone who has no idea what they're getting into?

Great interviews give ample time for both parties to ask qualification questions. This means you as a job candidate need to be just as prepared to grill the hiring manager as he/she is prepared to grill you. The fact is, as much as you may think you want a job, you'll quickly change your mind if you turn over a few stones and discover some surprising deal-breaker facts about the job.

So, what are some great questions to ask your potential employer? Here's a list of ten questions we'd recommend you ask every time:

1. What have other employees done to succeed in this position?
2. What is the average rate of job turnover in this position? The company as a whole?
3. What do you most like - and least like - about working for this company?
4. What is your management style, and how will we communicate with each other on a daily basis if I am hired?

5. What training is provided to employees during and after onboarding? Are there any other resources employees are provided with for ongoing development and success?
6. If I am hired, how will my performance be measured and evaluated over time? What specific factors will be looked at most carefully?
7. How many people who have started in this position have been promoted within their first five years?
8. What are the biggest challenges I will face in this position in the first year if I'm hired?
9. Tell me about the company culture - how do people interact, do you guys schedule company events inside or outside of work, what's the vibe around the office?
10. Do you have any hesitations about my qualifications or experience?

8. Plan Your Transit Route in Advance

This goes along with showing up ten minutes early to the interview, but is important enough to include here as its own topic. You *must* plan your transit route to the interview in advance - and ideally, practice it at least once prior to your interview (and at the same time of day, on the same day of the week, so you know what to expect).

Mapping out your transit route in advance gives you a clear idea when you need to leave your house, or current place of work, to get to the interview on time. Practicing the route in advance additionally ensures you'll be aware of anything unusual, such as:

- Unexpected delays or traffic.
- Road construction and detours.

- How to handle parking in their lot, building, or off-site upon arrival.
- Where important navigational structures are located - front door, elevators, etc.
- Learning of any discrepancies in the address or location you have for the interview.

Remember, interviews are important and it pays to be prepared. You'll feel terrible if you wind up arriving late and blowing your shot at a great job just because you didn't take the time to plan this out ahead of time.

9. Know Your Strengths and Weaknesses

Whether you're applying for a technical job, sales job, administrative job, or something else altogether, it pays to know your strengths and weaknesses. There is no need to conceal your weaknesses, but of course you will want to play your strengths - and highlight those things you feel make you stand out above the crowd.

In order to get a real, objective handle on your strengths and weaknesses, there are three steps we recommend you take.

First, make your own lists of your personal strengths and weaknesses as you see them. Be as honest with yourself as possible, thinking of your top five best and worst qualities. Now practice describing these qualities during an interview.

In the case of your strengths, you want to be sure not to come off as arrogant or egotistical, but still highlight your strongest abilities. This is often best done by *telling a story*. For example, rather than outright stating that you're great at customer service, you might illustrate your strengths in action by discussing that one time you managed to calm down an irate customer over the phone, not only keeping their business, but even up-selling them on a larger package that would better meet their needs!

In the case of your weaknesses, you want to make sure you don't paint yourself as an incompetent worker, but you still need to be honest. Everyone has weaknesses and it can be insincere to try to frame your weaknesses as strengths (i.e., *"my greatest weakness is that I work too hard…"*). Our best recommendation here is that you discuss weaknesses which are not of critical impact to the job.

For example, if you are applying for an accounting job, it would be a deal-breaker if you don't have good attention to detail - and frankly, you shouldn't want to apply to a job that doesn't match your strengths anyways. If you're applying for a sales job, though, attention to detail might not be as critical as people-skills, so admitting that you're not a spreadsheet wizard probably isn't the end of the world.

Second, get feedback on your self-composed list of strengths and weaknesses from friends, family, and colleagues. Others will often see traits in us that we cannot see ourselves, so it can really pay to obtain this outside perspective. You may realize some really great strengths of yours that you had previously overlooked, and you may also realize you had some blind spots where you really need to improve.

As an added bonus, people providing an outside perspective will usually explain their opinion by providing an example of a time you displayed that strength/weakness. As discussed earlier, it is often helpful to illustrate your strengths by telling stories - so getting this outside perspective may help you find great stories to tell that you otherwise wouldn't have considered.

Third, consider obtaining [a professional assessment of your behavioral and motivational strengths and weaknesses](). This is something our firm can provide at a reduced cost for job applicants, and it can be extremely helpful for the sake of interviewing.

By understanding where you are likely to err with your communication ahead of time, you can avoid stepping on landmines that might hurt your chances of landing the job. Furthermore, you can apply your assessment insights to understand your interviewer's behavioral style and tailor your communication towards it - demonstrating great verbal skills and collaboration abilities, and showing through your actions that you work and communicate well with others.

Since every company is looking to hire people who are team players and easy to get along with, understanding your unique behavioral style and motivators can give you a decisive edge during job interviews.

10. Learn How Body Language Affects Communication

Imagine a great leader giving a public speech at a podium.

There she is, maintaining excellent posture and eye contact. Furthermore, she is using her hands to reinforce her points while she talks, and speaks from her diaphragm for clear and powerful speech. Her movements are balanced, remaining active with her body without being jumpy - her movements are purposeful and paced, adding to the weight of her message without being distracting.

How would this leader be perceived, though, if her movements *were* jumpy and distracting? Or at the opposite end of the spectrum, if she stood still - dead as a rock? In either case it would be more difficult to pay attention to her, understand her message, and even to take her seriously.

This is because 90% of communication is nonverbal. In fact, the majority of our communication comes through our body language. After this, the next most important factor in communication is our tone of voice. Finally, the words we actually speak only convey about 10% of the overall message we're sending to someone at any point in time.

For these reasons, your entire body, mind, and emotions need to be aligned in order to convey the *same* message across all spheres of verbal and nonverbal communication. If these spheres are not in congruence with one another, others will struggle to understand your message and may subconsciously question your authenticity.

This is actually a big reason most hiring managers want to meet you in person prior to hiring you. It gives them a chance to let their subconscious or "gut" evaluate you beyond the words. It allows them the opportunity to scan and analyze anything that seems shady, out-of-order, or strange.

How do you align all three spheres of your verbal and nonverbal communication, though? How do you work on constructing powerful, congruent nonverbal messages to accompany the words you speak? The answer is simple: practice.

Practice in front of the mirror, practice with friends, and practice with family. If you really want to get serious about it, you can even consider signing up for an acting class! During such classes, you'll get hands-on feedback from an instructor who is specifically evaluating you on these factors.

You might also consider investing in private body language training, whether that's reading some books or taking an online course. This isn't for everyone, but it can make a lifelong impact if you do spend the time learning the fundamentals.

For now, here are eight quick tips you can use to make an immediate improvement to your body language:

- Maintain good eye contact, but don't stare. Looking away every now and then is okay.
- Keep good posture while sitting and standing. Think: straight back, head held high, arms open.
- Avoid crossing your arms or legs, which subconsciously signals disapproval or hesitation.
- Have a great attitude, smiling and laughing when appropriate.
- Lean in a little bit when the other person is talking, and tilt your head to one side to indicate a deep interest in what they're saying.

- Don't fidget, tap your hands or feet, or touch your face.
- Relax your shoulders and arms, and be comfortable taking up some space. Making yourself "bigger" is a display of confidence and relaxation, whereas making yourself "smaller" is a sign of uncertainty and tension.
- Use your hands to supplement your speech, especially while sitting.

11. Follow Up with a Prompt "Thank You"

Sending a thank you card or email is a powerful way to end the interview process. When the hiring manager receives a handwritten card from you with some thoughtful remarks a few days after the interview, you will immediately be put at the front of their mind. Emails don't have the same personal touch, but are still a good substitute if sending a physical card isn't possible or practical.

Thank you cards alone won't win you a job, but they are an expected formality at many places of business. Those candidates who do send thank you cards demonstrate their ability to follow up, too, showing they are conscientious. In a situation where a hiring manager is having a tough time deciding between two candidates, a thank you card just might be what you need to set yourself apart from the other person.

It's also important to realize how few people still say "please" and "thank you" in this modern day and age. Because of this, you can distinguish yourself simply by making a point of doing this with others. Be the person who says please and thank you consistently. It is a worthwhile sign of respect, consideration, and sophistication.

12. Have a Balanced View of the Outcome

When you are applying for jobs, it pays to remember that it's not a life-or-death situation. If you don't get a particular job, the sun will still rise tomorrow. Sure, it may be a little disappointing, but rejection is a part of life and there's no point getting hung up on it. Keep a smile on your face and realize that if something wasn't meant to be, there isn't any point in forcing it.

Every job you apply to is an opportunity to advance your career, but not every job will be a great fit for you. In fact, even jobs that you think would be a great fit often aren't - remember, 80% of the workforce is basically unhappy in their current position for one reason or another.

For these reasons, getting turned down from a job can be just as useful and positive as being made an offer. What if that job you'd wanted *did* make you an offer, but it was a poor fit - and what if you'd accepted it and become miserable? Worse yet, what if you took that job and missed an even greater opportunity as a result?

Getting turned down from a job also means you *tried* - which is far better than sitting back and doing nothing. In order to reach your goals in life, career or otherwise, you need to take consistent action of them to sustain progress.

While getting turned down may not be ideal, it's a real life feedback sign that you are doing just that - taking action towards your goals. If anything, you deserve a pat on the back for being courageous enough to put yourself out there and take the risk.

During your job hunt, then, remember that there are plenty of fish in the sea. Just because one company didn't hire you doesn't mean there isn't an even better opportunity right around the corner. In fact, there almost always is if you keep your head up and stay in the game. We know you will do great!

Conclusion

It's my mission to increase the number of great job matches between employers and employees. At my consulting firm [ThinkPlanLaunch](), we work with employers to put people into the right jobs so they can be successful, happy, and fulfilled. Moreover, this allows companies to improve their bottom line and more easily reach their business goals.

Therefore, it is my sincere hope that you took something valuable away from this book. Perhaps you realized something important you otherwise wouldn't have realized, or perhaps you finally got the motivation to solicit some much-needed feedback from your friends, family, and co-workers (which is really a powerful exercise, honestly - don't skip it!).

In closing, please feel free to contact me via my personal website with any questions you might have, as I would be happy to answer them.

Finally, please consider leaving an honest review of this book online. Whether you loved the book or not, it would be incredibly helpful to obtain your unbiased feedback.

Thank you again for purchasing this book and best of luck in your job hunt!

www.ingramcontent.com/pod-product-compliance
Lightning Source LLC
Chambersburg PA
CBHW020709180526
45163CB00008B/3008